Make Angels in the Snow

Make Angels in the Snow

Thoughts/Prayers regarding Angels in Poetic Form

(Warning: Beware of these angels.
Their loving and inquisitive nature can be contagious.)

Paul E. Stiffler

To order additional copies of this book, contact:
Xlibris Corporation
1-888-795-4274
www.Xlibris.com
Orders@Xlibris.com
64283

This dedication is made to the following:

To Elsie, my wife, who worked tirelessly beside me to bring thoughts, prayers, and love to the pages of this book.

To our children and their families: daughter Cheryl and Bob Nelson and son Jonathan and Roxanne. To our grandchildren: Michelle and husband Joe Thompson; Kyle Stiffler; Jennifer, David, and Robert Nelson; Amy and Jason Otterness; and Jared Scanlon. To our great-grandchildren: Joelle Otterness and Colby Thompson. They keep us young and looking forward.

I recognize that this effort was done in an environment of affectionate support and good cheer. The staff at First Congregational Church fills the hallways with energy, boundless commitment, and laughter. To these colleagues in ministry, I give my love and admiration:

To Rich Kirchherr, the energetic and wise senior pastor, who is outstanding in bringing the Word to refresh our hearts; to Leslie Ritter-Jenkins, minister of discipleship, whose deep commitment to intellectual and spiritual pursuits opens a world of inspiration; to Meredith Onion, our associate in pastoral care, who brings energy and wisdom to all in need; to Jan Fraccaro, director of Christian education, who lovingly guides our children to understand Christ's presence in the world; to Mike Tilden, director of youth ministries, who mobilizes the imagination of youth into several missions; and to Debbie Stankiewicz, our parish nurse, who watches over all of us and the congregation with gentle and loving care.

Support, understanding, and patient guidance are the qualities that connect us and are given by Mary Jo McKeag, Meg Heinz, Amy Baldwin, Linda Conlin, Lori O'Neil, Amy Faison, Chuck Cavanaugh, and Felipe Hernandez.

Inspiration for our hearts and souls is provided by our music staff: Kathy Christian, organist; Ray Klemchuk, music director; Debbie Mairs, youth choir; Amy Shropshire, children's choirs; K. C. Congdon, bell choir; Lana Wordel, steel drum band; and Brian Clarke, spirit worship band.

Foreword

"Somewhere between the mundane and the divine lies metaphor." That quote from Plato reminds me of Paul's poems and his ministry in our midst. Paul has brought to our congregation in Western Springs a piece of the spiritual puzzle that was missing. The labyrinth, his "breathing prayers," a mystical understanding of head and heart coming together in faith, services of healing and anointing—these are just a few examples of the manifold gifts to which Paul has introduced us. Most important of all, however, has been Paul's pastoral care through worship. Paul has helped us to glimpse the divine in the quotidian rhythms and patterns of our lives in the poems and sermons that he weaves with music.

Consider these poems to be Paul's offering to both God and God's people. Some of them are personal, others communal. Some of them celebrate joyous anniversaries, and others honor the end of life. But each is a glimpse of the divine spirit of love made accessible through the gift of words and metaphor.

Here's my recommendation: Do not sit down to read this book cover to cover. It's not a novel with an introduction, character, and situational development. No, I think the best way to encounter this book is poem by poem, glimpse by glimpse, day by day. Pick a month or season—a time of joy or a time of challenge—and let the poems of this book wash over you day by day. Most of all, read these musings as I believe they were intended as a gift to God and to you.

Dr. Richard Kirchherr, Senior Pastor
First Congregational Church of Western Springs

Informative Facts

About the Author's Work

About the Angels

About Poetry/Prayers

Inspirational Thoughts

From Nature
From Celebrations
From Encouragement
From Remembering
From Inspired Moments

PREFACE

While on my way to a retreat, I suddenly pulled the car to the side of the road and wrote, in its full form, the words "do angels fly?" It was as though I was merely the recorder of thoughts that came from the universe, a convergence of an ethereal sense of presence far beyond any experienced before, uniting with words familiar to my mind. It became a soul question, pondering beyond curiosity the ambiance of a deepening spirituality. It was healing more than anything else.

Do Angels Fly? written on May 5, 2000, was the first of the angel poems and is published in an anthology by the International Society of Poets.

As more and more angel poems came into being, some of the same images experienced at the onset presented themselves although there were more and varied presences. Each angel poem relates to earthly incidence in the lives of those for whom I give pastoral care. Often, the poem shapes itself before any contact is made. After I send it, responses indicate how needful or how intuitive the poem was for that person.

Each poem is a lived experience through me for someone. I live them too, for the angels who sponsor them are real to me. Angels bring grace and merciful healing, lifting us to a higher realm.

Gardens of Hope was written for the International Society of Poets Convention and Symposium in Washington DC on August 15-17, 2003. It was added to the World's Longest Poem for Peace (according to *Guinness*).

Some poems will be recognized by attendees at a spiritual retreat held by our parish nurse, Debbie Stankiewicz. At her request, the poems were given with a personal note to each of the recipients.

I have added personal poems to my wife (for all these poems are love poems of some sort) to illustrate that one's heartbeat can send music to another and to our life together that is nearing sixty years.

Make Angels in the Snow has been revised and is now the title of this book. It is one that my wife and I especially favor. If there is enough snow,

I suggest you stop reading, don your winter garments, and go outside, then make an angel in the snow! If the calendar does not present snow, find a puffy cloud formation, lie back, and let the angel form. Now read the poem that brought my thoughts into reality.

Make Angels in the Snow

O my soul,
Make Angels in the snow,
Leave imprints of Divine attention,
For our lives are bleak with woe.
On layered cold from heaven's sky,
Make Angels in the snow.

Sweep arms and legs in circles wide,
Cover landscapes with heart's tradition,
Pattern the earth on every side,
Make angels in the snow.

Appear once more and sing again,
And tell of peace, goodwill,
Remember songs with sweet refrain,
Make Angels in the snow.

Bring magic to the souls of men,
Courage to right our wrong,
Let one brave act of hope portend,
Make angels in the snow.

For God, to us his grace now lending,
Invite a child to make it so,
For they with God's great joy now sending,
Make Angels in the snow.

ABOUT THE ANGELS

Fun—that's what these angels are. Playful companions, healing workers, as well as doorways to mysterious realms. Open this book and expect to find these entities touching your life. Perhaps you will find yourself swinging high into the sky as you did when you were a child or, as the title suggests, making an angel in the snow.

If, by chance, you are facing the rigors of illness or deep sadness, you might experience, at least for a moment, a healing lift. If these things take place, then my pastoral inclinations will have been worthwhile; this is the way of my heart. In language beyond ordinary conversation, I reach into the ethereal world when life cannot be explained or understood. Puzzles in life remain, but ultimately, we expect to see them as a completed picture.

The Bible names two archangels: Gabriel, meaning "God is my strength," and Michael, meaning "who is God?" They are found in the biblical book of Daniel, the Gospels of Luke and Jude, and Revelation. Michael is considered the greatest of all angels in Judaism, Christianity, and Islam. Two other prominent angels in the field of angel lore are Raphael and Uriel. Raphael, meaning "God has healed," is of Chaldean origin and is named in the book of Tobit. Uriel means "fire of God," and it is suggested that he was the angel who fought with Jacob at Peniel. Understand, however, that none of these are the angels to which I refer.

Many books can be found on personal experiences of angels. This is not the intent of *Make Angels in the Snow*. Nor is it an attempt to develop a theology about angels although some may see it this way. Rather, these are moments that occurred at a particular time, each one being a separate experience, such as "Ode to a Little Chapel." With meditative thought and prayer, they were written as a response of pastoral care or inspiration for a time and place, as in "On a Beautiful April Day," while looking out my office window. (This is one of those poems that knits itself together.) That is what I do; that is what I am. And in some situations, that is how I think, pray, and write.

Pastoral care is a discipline providing a full range of opportunity. I observe members in our hallways speaking with compassion to one another or, with permission, stepping into a person's worst shift-of-life moment with soup and bread or silently sitting with someone in an untenable and heartbreaking moment.

Scampy little cherubs please the heart and mind. If you wish to invoke an image of angels while reading these poems, then by all means, do so. The words herein address a particular human situation(s). Some of them are personal; they may match your own experience. One could think of them as words where no word can avail itself. Being speechless before serious matters that life imposes upon us is common. We can but shake our heads at the things that shake us.

An understandable way to look upon these poems is as a pastoral effort to embrace life as it happens with loving care. It can be an invitation for October's blue sky to join us at the junction where imagination and reality meet, a joining of where our pilgrimage takes us. In the great surround of God's beauty, an entity other than our earthly life gives flight to fear and sorrow. We can, for a brief span of time, be taken away from harsh turns of life, which disillusion us, and become whole, even for a moment.

Enjoy and be carried away; you will always return.

ABOUT THE POETRY/PRAYERS

Prayer is personal. Written in a poetic form, some of the prayers that follow are for specific occasions, that is, great joy as when I wrote a prayer/poem for my great-grandson before he was born, known then as Baby T and now as Colby Robert. Another entry is for Maria and Anthony Caselli, who were then expecting their first child. Michael Andrew is now three years old. Others are happy moments, as in the poems for my wife on our fifty-fifth anniversary, and now we're married for fifty-nine years. In addition, there are poems that delve into the depths of sorrow in personal loss as well as the heights of faith and hope. These are found in the poems and tributes written for Catherine Louise Price.

Inspiration is caught in a poem written for Hazel Teichen about a chapel that she transformed into a beautiful place of residence, a home with comfort and many touches that became "a surprise for the eye." After selling, she continues her creative life in other venues.

In "A Garden of the Heart," sorrow and love are felt due to the closing of a beautiful, flowering, and flourishing nursery operated by two good friends, Debbie and Scott Grosse. The nursery was opened with a poem/blessing, which is included here.

A tribute to Emily, a thirteen-year-old girl who was accidentally struck and killed by a truck while walking across the street with her bicycle, was written for her family. Her father, a Muslim, and her mother, a Methodist, gathered with their imam, me, and friends for a memorial service at First Congregational Church of Western Springs. Emily, an elegant, happy child, had a wish for which she prayed: that all peoples of faith would be one. It was the way she lived.

An additional poem, "Thoughts on Plum Lake," is included because of a deeply inspiring moment.

All the enclosed poetry center around the human spirit: celebrating, encouraging, remembering, and inspiring as we move through the experience of life on earth.

Inspirational Thoughts

From Nature

Divine Clay 23
On a Beautiful April Day 24
Creation II..25
Summer Angels...26
Summer Stars 27
I Remember September..28
Thoughts on Plum Lake 29
Angel Brushes 31
Sweet Angels Come 32
To a Thirteenth Moon 33
Listen to the Wind...34

From Celebrations

Bethlehem Angels 39
Birthday..40
To Baby T...41
A New Song 43
A House Blessing..44
Ode to a Little Chapel 45
Millennium 2000..46
To *My* Beloved Wife Elsie 48
To the Valentine Heart...49
Happy Anniversary...50

From Encouragement

My Heart Sings...55
Come Fly with Me...56

Soul Vision..57
Warm Embrace 58
Angels of Mystery 59
Asking 60
A Touch of Incarnation 61
Dancing Births 62
As One 63
My Heart an Open Sky...64

From Remembering

Send Out Doves 69
Longing...70
Flowering Beauty 71
A Garden of the Heart...72
Spirit of Love 73
An Angel among Us...74
      Sing to My Heart 75
      Adorning 76
      Sunshine Angels 77
      A Tribute 78
Peace...79
Mystery 80

From Inspired Moments

Prayer...85
Soul Romancing 86
Beloved...87
Ice-alations 88
Meeting Janus...89
Gardens of Hope 90
A World Prays 91
Listen for Angel Songs...92

Inspirational Thoughts

From Nature

Divine Clay
On a Beautiful April Day
Creation II
Summer Angels
Summer Stars
I Remember September
Thoughts on Plum Lake
Angel Brushes
Sweet Angels Come
To a 13th Moon
Listen to the Wind

DIVINE CLAY

Angels of our earthenware,
come to me, I pray,
that I may know as once before,
when birthing earth began
and love my heart was thus inscribed:
O gentle breath of God,
fragrance is your presence,
sunbeams dancing o'er my head, your
embrace,
soft moonlight, your tenderness,
deep blues of night, your gentle rest,
raindrops gently tapping my face, your
love.
How could I ever miss you
when you surround me so?

On a Beautiful April Day

I saw you, gracious Angels dear
Playing in the garden near
Swaying with each daff'dil flower
There beneath the stately tower
Stepping lightly 'mid stirring leaves
With your Spring as Winter grieves.
I saw you, gracious Angels dear
Calling children far and near
Brushing cheeks as soft as down
With red and blue and green and brown.
For in your mirthful, prankish way
No bitter cold can now hold sway
As tiny little noses run
Smiles abound in heavenly fun.
I saw you, gracious Angels dear
I only ask that you draw near
To me who holds a child within
Who rushes out to play and win
The prize of Spring with air so fresh
That heart and mind and soul doth mesh
And seize the gift of living joy
Returning now as girl and boy.
I saw you, gracious Angels dear
I know now that you did draw near
For I have found my child set free
With boundless hope and laughing glee.

Creation II

Beginning all beginnings
Love dwelt in deepest universe.
Blackened holes and swirling galaxies
Deadened stars and planets spinning
Captured by divine embrace
Moved in orderly awe.
No less that redeeming reach
In dark earth caves Love's trace.
Never loosed from tender hold
As grave clothes tightly bind
And cold departs by spirit's glow
Stirs One whose steps were bold.
Oh, come forth, thou Love divine
I wait in sorrow's colorless wake
For angels to sing some new song.
I long for mercy to be mine
O majestic and unending Love
Move into my heart, I implore.
Give life where once my soul had died
Bring resurrecting breath from glory above.

SUMMER ANGELS

Summer angels,
swing in my childlike heart,
playground of my soul,
rising above the earth,
looking into the sky,
air pushing against my face,
falling downward, backward,
touching close to earth's breast,
seeing the sky,
seeing the earth,
seeing the sky,
seeing the earth,
gaining momentum of thrill
with each backward rising,
ground rushing up,
and passing by,
as heaven greets with beauty.
O the rising,
O the falling,
O the swinging,
O the living!

Summer Stars

Guide the stars of summer,
celestial angels.
Send their scintillating beams
with calm and steady course,
cooling earth's feverish brow.

In darkest night hold light
against the pitch of war
and worse,
the drought of souls
dried by weariness of heart.

Prevail in starvation's fierce endeavor,
its howling hunger pains,
the source
of children's play abandoned,
their energy denied them.

Ignite the souls that look beyond,
star searchlights now revealing,
far beyond remorse,
sparkling ways restoring earth
and children's eyes like stars to shine.

Stars of summer's eve assure me,
streaking planets tell
of kindness rising up with force
as restless dreams hold forth
a world enough, a world at peace.

(After finishing the book *Enough* by Roger Thurow and Scott Kilman about the struggle to end hunger through the efforts of African and American farmers with major corporations and individuals.)

I Remember September

She stood on hilltops
October winds brushing her sweet face
Blending her hair with the colors of fall
Caressing lips waiting to be kissed
Gently
Sweeping elegance embraced by sunlight
Pouring its heated love deeply within
Stars from afar shifting their course
Gazing with rapture at earth's beauty
Wrapping the arms of love around
Touching where no one has touched
Joyful union of infinity with all that is finite
A moment without time or space
Single eternity with brief time
Forever lasting
Forever divine.

Thoughts on Plum Lake

Roll in, thou quiet drifting fog
soften in your mysterious way
silhouettes of island, bog
touch every shore and every bay.

Break in, thou sunshine, drink the dew
pull back the gentle cords of morn
your mystic deepening love renew
as first when all this land was born.

Caressing wind, O, sail my soul
that I may glide across this lake
to wonders where my heart will bow
and there in awe and wonder wake.

With calm and cooling waters heal
wounds from living out my dream
immerse in stillness life more real
my soul as fabric without seam.

Waves play the music of my breath
soothe heartbeat with surprise to see
praying trees of height and breadth
cool, shadowed paths to love's decree.

With calmer waves of evening tide
reveal deep secrets since your time
to now with elegant mirth abide
within each rolling kiss sublime.

Thou rhythmic palette of sunrise, set
reflect the colors of even morn.
Glorify God who made and let
ecstatic passions thus be born.

Draw close the leaves, a blanket form
and snuggle in a restful fall
well done through summer rain and storm
breathing your breath of life for all.

Through winter's coverlet of snow
give warmth to creatures down below
spring, like my soul, thus rise to know
new wonders once again bestow.

From hidden depths bring healing peace
for those whom once you dearly held
give sorrow's troubled breast release
love in place where once they dwelled.

Oh, wonder's still and graceful way
witness to a thousand dreams
thrill each heart that gasps dismay
with fantasies from fairy beams.

Touch with cooling balm my shore
in your alluvion manner soft
as in your legendary days of yore
my seeking dove is sent aloft.

Sweet angels voice this earnest sigh
that I would reach beyond all seeing
when heaven bows from out the sky
then my soul will leap to being.

(An early morning sponsored by the angel wings of fog at Camp Highlands for Boys, Sayner, Wisconsin, July 2007)

ANGEL BRUSHES

You sweep with lovely colors rare
Across earth's supple breast
Clothing with brilliance all that's bare
A sign of Nature's rest.

Sweet autumn's golden maiden fair
Bring color to my soul
With angel brushes paint with flair
As changing winds take toll.

When slowly fades the color green
And other hues take place
Browns inherit the earth now lean
Come first in winter's race.

Color with flourish all things red
Add yellow to the edge
Or orange's majesty instead
With flowers on each hedge.

My heart awaits your angel change
As seasons come and go
My soul would need peace arrange
Love's seed of mercy sows.

O, sweep with lovely colors rare
This waiting heart of mine
O, harvest from my soul to share
From all God's store divine.

Sweet Angels Come

Sweet angels come,
part the clouds of wistfulness
that October's blue would stream
into my life again
writing new melodies
not heard by my heart before
yet lingering with notes
of Creator's love.
Declare with winged softness
all that waits for me
for which I was born
to which I move
alert to your surprise.
Fan embers now lying, dying
so fire might burst forth
as once I knew
that which you see
always as new.
Brush against my face
with your angel wings
cooling and healing
the ravishes of present moments
that dreams would step forth
from worlds still untapped
my love as God creates it to be.

To a Thirteenth Moon

Thou
Bright and full moon
     heavy with love messages,
     eons of sighs,
     all seeing,
     all hearing,
     all knowing.

Creator's appointee for watchful rounds
Scanning night and day divides,
What do you know?
What do you hear?
What do you see?
Peering into this night?
     Do sighs remind you of first love?
     Do words remind you of first sound?
     Do melodies remind you of first song?

     I am the one who
          sighs
             speaks
        and sings.

Look once more in lunarian brightness,
O feminine beauty of the skies,
Thou holder of dreams,
Do my moments remind you of first love?

LISTEN TO THE WIND
(OR AND SPEAKING OF LOVE)

Listen to the wind
Speaking of love,
Gently caressing your face
With the language of a gentle touch,
Soothing,
Smoothing surfaces of sadness,
Whispering,
Which only the heart can hear,
Words of passionate longing
As in a universe
Only for you.
Listen to the wind
As it carries music
Romancing the soul,
Honeymoon
In angel realms,
Blessedness.

Inspirational Thoughts

From Celebrations

Bethlehem Angels
Birthday
To Baby T
A New Song
A House Blessing
Ode to a Little Chapel
Millennium
To *My* Beloved Wife
To the Valentine Heart
Happy Anniversary

Bethlehem Angels

Bethlehem angels, sing out again
      make of that long-past yesterday
this day of mine that I may gain
      from echoed hillsides on display;
send stars and brilliance as of God.

"Fear not!" you sing out to my soul
      spread your joyful song
lest fear becomes night's reaching toll
      and wholeness lost for which I long;
send stars and brilliance as of God.

Show the way to Beth'lem's child
      born to set me free
announce to fill this winter mild
      with visions of healing yet to be;
send stars and brilliance as of God.

Fly above o'er all the earth
      angels of mercy sweet and kind
show the place for love's new birth
      humanity with grace to bind;
send stars and brilliance as of God.

Carry with this prayer of mine
      celestial healing for all the earth
touch my body, soul, and mind
      in these days of second birth;
send stars and brilliance as of God.

Birthday

And God's angels gathered round
'Mid fluttering wings, angelic sound
You ponder the earth, O thou Great Love
What send you forth from this above?

"I bring to life a tender heart
And give to her a special part
Of all that I have made to be
Beyond the work of land and sea
Not seen but only known a bit
When spirits touch and all things fit."

You look and see all that will come
Though soul will leave its lovely home?

"I see the course my precious child
Must walk across the desert wild
So I endow my greatest gift
To her whose spirit comes to lift
Those who follow the path before
Where heartache leaves the soul but sore
I send to earth an ethereal mist
To freely live a life not missed
Embracing with her very charm
To keep my own from every harm.
I send thee forth ethereal mist
So by thy life earth will be blessed."

To Baby T

Angels of God's birthing breath,
attend my day of coming.
Fill my heart with joyful mirth,
Attend with care my 'waited birth.

Grant to mother your tender touch,
to Father your steady presence,
wisdom both of mind and heart,
to her who guides God's skill impart.

Awaken me to worlds now giv'n,
come soothe my crying venture,
let body, soul, and mind begin
a life of love and hope to win.

Throughout the days that lie ahead,
be with my heart and soul.
Open doors on paths to tread
that all in time will lead to God.

O angels of discerning love,
grant my body to be strong,
fit my mind to be awake,
strong in heart to walk love's gait.

Make of my soul a living room,
where I invite you to dwell,
for God shall be my steady guest
as I complete my given quest.

Great-grandfather Paul
July 15, 2009

(Looking out on Plum Lake, Camp Highlands for Boys, Sayner, Wisconsin)

Born 08-08-09 at Chicago, Illinois, weighing at 9.6 pounds and
23.6 inches long
Named Colby Robert Thompson

A New Song

Send watchful care, O angels sweet
Hover o'er this child of mine
Warm the body head to feet
You who know our God divine.

Fill my heart with songs you know
Soothe this child with womblike warmth
And when in birthing head would show
Bring ease and shelter from all harm.

For now in God's appointed round
I bring creation's wondrous gift
To life where love and hope abound
And ne'er from God would ever drift.

I pray thee now Creator God
As your angels spread their wing
When baby feet will touch earth's sod
And find your song to ever sing.

Give health and hope to body, soul
Mercies give to that first breath
In healing love where all is whole
Tiny heart beats till life's death.

In this season of destiny
Now I play in gardens joy
Love from here to eternity
Bring forth a girl, perhaps a boy.

My heart rejoices as of old
When Mary's heart sang your praise
My voice will sing forever bold
My soul, its love forever raise.

(For Maria and Andrew Caselli, then waiting for their first child. Michael
Anthony is now three years old.)

A House Blessing

O Holy God,
    Grant your angels spread their wings
        o'er this home and hearts now joining
        of love and nurturing care would sing
        where beauty and sacred trust are showing.

    Spread the wings of your protection
        from fiercest winds and storms assailing
        gather by your will's intention
        all their secret prayers fulfilling.

    Cover ills and hopes prevailing
        with your mighty power above
        hold their hearts and souls sustaining
        Grace forgive with healing love.

    With wings of kindness always hov'ring
        o'er prayers of gratefulness and need
        blessed hope be always showering
        upon these lives your mercy speed.

    With your angels' wings surrounding
        hold the precious gift of life
        of this refuge harbor making
        burdens ceasing, rest from strife.

    May all who enter find a blessing
        as they who live here truly find
        peace and joy and hope professing
        with godly love all hearts do bind.

    We pray thee listen to souls now pleading
        that they would find in dark of night
        solace where body and soul are mending
        and peaceful sleeping in Christ's light. Amen.

Ode to a Little Chapel

Angels of passionate love
How could I pass by
When you lifted the veil
And all surroundings became transparent?
How was it that my heart stood still
When in but a moment I saw beyond
Stone and brick and mortar
A dream hurtling from creation
Grabbing my soul
Flooding my heart with rampant thoughts?
Angels of glorious love
It was you who transformed its setting
Placing outside of traffic dust and noise
Idyllic peacefulness and serene eternity
Beckoning weariness to find rest
Sadness to find joy
Emptiness to be filled.
All the time just sitting there
Waiting
Waiting
Waiting for me
To heal my soul with true calling.
I furnish you with my complete love
Body, heart, mind, and soul
Little chapel—just sitting there.

(Written for Hazel Teichen, who transformed a small chapel in
LaGrange, Illinois, into a glorious home for the heart where prayers still
linger, July 2005)

Millennium 2000
For my Elsie with love

"For a thousand years in thy sight are but as yesterday when it is past, and as a watch in the night" (Psalm 90:4).

It did not take long at all, a twinkling of your eye in fact, and all earthly creation was ushered into this new thousand-year dimension of time marked for our own means and not for things divine.

On this eve, there came, without notice, a divine moving of all matters spiritual. Animals continued their concert to the moon, night growing moved on under dark blankets of soft and wonderful care, nudged from sleep to continue the vast network of flora-sustaining life, foresting needs of survival, and rest coming with slumbering dreams. And our hearts did throb at its wonder. Humankind, having chosen the quieter middle of night to the blaring middle of day, illuminated the heavens in grandiose displays encircling the planet with shouts and welcome, exercising each brief span of life to enlarge their fraction of history into a momentous privilege of being in the context of measured time, a line drawn to call attention to passing seasons, notable events, and more importantly, the observation of love quickly moving out of reach, carried on to ethereal homelands, habitations of utmost love, having been released for quick journeys to other worlds, wherever they may be, never shaking from Creator's bond until it is realized once more and time no longer matters.

Falling ash from light displays, dances slowing to tired steps, mystery settling deeper in regions of soul to be called upon as days move across a calendar surface, and always the clean up along with waiting for another day, and then another, and then another until the abode of all saints ignites in some invented revelry for the grandeur of being here at all as short as it may be, secretly admitting to enduring love with love set free in rhythmic harmonies.

Everything is new; nothing goes on as it was before. Mystery remains with its mesmerizing call to join larger jubilees of heart and soul, heavenly hosts watching and, unnoticed, joining with our hands in dramatic seizing of Creator's gift, breath of life, earth journey. "Glory to God in the highest, and on earth peace . . ."

January 1, 2000

To My Beloved Wife Elsie (Fifty-five years)

It was you who brought forth
A garden in my life
Bringing colors of hope and blossoms of love
Carefully tending to the thirst
So needed to stay alive,
Placing hope when sun would burn
And droughts prevail
Nourishing me through times of wilted soul
Gasping for waters to penetrate hardened earth
Where I had chosen my life to be.

It was you who called attention
To glorious creation
Changing landscapes to God's appointed way
Where dawn forever splits open each night
And softer sunsets radiate eternal promise.
It was you who believed when all was parched
And little could be seen as life moved on
All things perennial returning time and again
While annuals gave beauty to yearly surprise.
It was you in all these years
That have come to be
Our family dear, and you and me.
I love you.

August 19, 2005

To the Valentine Heart

Over the years when mountains seemed insurmountable
and rivers too deep to cross,
when sunlight disappeared
behind the clouds of my own making
as though there was only darkness in which to walk,
of this I could be sure,
your love layered upon our love,
as snow falls upon snow.

When each season acted as the one before
or the one to follow,
unpredictable and with drastic change,
so much like the moods of my early days,
on this one truth I could depend,
your love layered upon our love,
as snow falls upon snow.

Now as years, like leaves in fall,
have dropped around us,
creating breathtaking art,
so you have managed our years
and made of home and heart,
a view of heaven yet to come,
I knew this above all else,
this constant act of healing love,
which changed my very being
was itself eternity
from no one else but you,
it was and still is
your love layered upon our love,
as snow falls upon snow.

Happy Anniversary

My heart doth float when you are near,
For all else fades and comes to naught,
Each pulse beat sings of you, my dear,
Throughout the years that time has wrought.

Could we but think of destiny,
When first we set our way,
That all would stretch eternity,
As love stays on, what may?

Angels of such tender love,
Hold fast our hearts, now old,
Bring peace below, each side, above,
For all is yet untold.

>To my beloved Elsie
>Fifty-ninth wedding anniversary
>August 19, 2009

Inspirational Thoughts

From Encouragement

My Heart Sings
Come Fly with Me
Soul Vision
Warm Embrace
Angels of Mystery
Asking
Tough of Incarnation
Dancing Births
As One
My Heart an Open Sky

My Heart Sings

Angels showering mercy
Blessings from on high
Restoring
Repairing
Renewing
No wonder my heart sings.
Loaning your wings
Lifting in flight
Burdened souls
In lowest moments
Pluck heartstrings
When there is no song.
Now in concert
With music of the spheres
Standing on the brink of creation
Everlasting dawn
Offering another first day
For God's anthem of joy
Echoes in the universe
It is good! It is good! It is good!

Come Fly with Me

Come fly with me in your angel sky
Sweet messenger of heaven.
Rest in the sanctuary of my heart.
Your watchful care, my peacefulness.
Nothing detains my soul now.
We soar together
Over clouds light and dark.
Your home where we sup
Is as lips kissing sweetly,
Dining divine energy,
Intoxicating love,
Rhythmic swaying of body being,
With exotic fruits;
Nothing earthbound stays my spirit
Dancing high
Beyond the reach of reason
Where only my heart knows.
Fly with me, oh angel heart.
We are as one.

Soul Vision

Did you see it
Angels of luxurious sweetness
While gracefully floating in and out
Of my heart's chambers
Where love is stored
Tenderly placed in each corner
Gently waiting for release
Upon unsuspecting sorrows
Madness spilled and flooding
Over broken souls
Longing still for peace?
Did you see its hesitation
Doubts rising up as ghosts
With old rejections
Wanting yet timid desires
To heal my beloved nation?
Did you feel the heat of passion
Daring and brave
Courage filled with dangers
Land of the free in some new fashion?
Did you see it
Angels that fill the sky
Sweeping through my soul
Feather touches bringing strength?
Did you see
The mystery I have yet to know?

Warm Embrace

Gathered in the warm embrace of presence,
Safe in your angel arms,
Before the glowing embers of rapture,
Hearts beating as one,
Loneliness is of no avail.
Cold slicing into flesh,
Numbing soul sorrows,
Melt away into rivers of balm,
Carrying away remorse
With the murmuring music
Of love's currents.
Transports to ecstasy and delight,
Worlds beyond worlds,
Universe open,
Accepting,
Welcoming,
As angels gather me in a warm embrace.

Angels of Mystery

My heart was empty
Hollow
Echoes of pain
Dropping heavily within
Wounds too tender to touch
Sharp punctured memories
Esteem in disarray
All seemed to stay
Until you
Angel of blessing
Held forth your soft hands
With delicate soothing of fingertips
Drawing across my flesh
Closed open infections of despair
Angel love of mysterious care
Lifting my soul
Changing the beat of my heart
Singing the song of love
Humming the universe
In depths where mysterious strings vibrate
Sensuously
Earthiness
Breathing once more.

Asking

Fashion my heart with lightness
Angels ever winging
singing.
Decorate with your flamboyant joy
and ceaseless merriment
my heart's chamber of secrets.
Dance fairy steps upon my sadness
swirl me in pirouettes of freedom
swinging round in dizzy bliss.
Circle my being as you skip through my space
that I might be gathered
securely
lovingly
in the arms of eternity
bound with thee
as before my days
when heaven was shared
and my heart was light
back then.
Oh, fashion my heart
as you knew me when.

A Touch of Incarnation

Bundled in infinite mercy,
Caressed by angels surround,
Swaddled in birthing cloths,
You breathe my daily living.
From eons to nanoseconds,
Infinity to earth time,
Everlasting to mortality,
Always in the arms of love.
I have everything yet need nothing,
Emptied yet filled,
Breathless,
Without words,
All that is
Converge as soul;
As you are so I am.

Dancing Births

Circle me with your dancing
Angels of joyful light.
Ring round my soul
With love's announcing
A birthing of wonder.

Bestow God's blessings
As at ragged manger beds
'Mid darkened ancient midnights
Upon this earthly blight
Which seeks to reign supreme.

Emit your sweet breath of song
Making fresh the very air I breathe
Each gasp opening gates to Eden
Though I will breathless be
Pure wholeness for which I long.

Rain love upon my heart so parched
As deserts dry and heated
Until this siege that has its hold
Is finally defeated, by miracles
Of which I do not know.

My body, weary, tired, cries out
As handmaidens often do
Of burdens little understood
When magnifying the Lord
In places once foretold.

Lift these barren shadows
O, take my hand, I pray
That I may ring with you
And give, as God most surely does
Birthing of love's new day.

As One

Angels winging through my heart
How long has your song
Carried through the universe
Till reaching through black holes
Into my heart?

Do you echo love's presence
Through streams of light
Strands golden bright
Or thunderous super novae
Shaking untold stars
Swirling galactic patterns
Outlines of design imagining?

What is my heart but of you
Enraptured and floating
Carried by your gentle wings
Moving as a zephyr round me
Through my body
Now transparent and eager
Gate of love standing wide
Open
Ready?

Angels winging through my heart
At last together
One as the other.

My Heart an Open Sky

Do angels fly
on currents of song
chambered notes from far-flung choirs
lifting heart and soul
as in my brokenness
and unfaith
discouragement reigning
displacing soul vows?

Is there a winging breeze
to fan embers of a
long-remembered fire
once burning in my chest?

Fly oh fly, angels
for my heart is an open sky
wing your way into my soul
with mending sweetness
making whole
what earth cannot
for I salute the One
whose love you bring.

Inspirational Thoughts

From Remembering

Send Out Doves
Longing
Flowering Beauty
A Garden of the Heart
Spirit of Love
An Angel among Us
    Sing to My Heart
    Adorning
    Sunshine Angels
    A Tribute
Peace
Mystery

Send Out Doves

Angels of mercy, cover the world
with eternal love.
Blanket the earth like snow
as you do when winter comes
to cool the heat of war.
Soften and make new
old familiar landscapes
parched and dusty
torn and shredded
smoke raising devastation
we have seen too long.

Cover the world with messengers of peace
make all things crisp and green.
Wrap meanness with gentleness
anger with kindness
hostility with quietness
bitterness with sweet tang
sweep away all things mean.

Cover the world with a rainbow.
Send doves throughout the sky.
Bring signs of hope again
that hate no more shall drench
our life designed to live in garden space
and wrench our hearts in death.
Announce on hills and mountaintops
in valleys far and wide
peace, goodwill has come once more
and all shall live side by side.

Longing

Draw near to this heated earth
Angels of mercy
Draw near to its fractured ways
So taken by demons of unrest.
Nourish the starving heart
That longs for kindness
Lift trudging souls beyond this dust
Their rounded shoulders burdened with sadness
To bluer skies and softer clouds
Where faces shine as stars
And life stands erect once more
Out of mud and mire
Face upward to mystery
Where you dwell with One
Who sends you with mercy
To this heated, drying earth
Parched for the sake of love.

Flowering Beauty

Grant your angels spread their wing
o'er this place of hearts now joining
of love and nurturing care would sing
where beauty and trust are showing.

Spread the wings of your protection
from fiercest winds and storms assailing
gather in your will's intention
all their secret prayers fulfilling.

Cover ills and hopes prevailing
with your mighty power above
hold each heart and soul sustaining
Grace forgive with healing love.

With wings of kindness always hovering
o'er prayers of gratefulness and need
blessings of hope be always showering
upon these lives your mercy speed.

With your angels' wings surrounding
hold each precious gift of life
of this refuge a harbor making
burdens ceasing and rest from strife.

May all who enter find a blessing
as those who work here truly find
peace and joy and hope professing
with godly love all hearts do bind.

We pray thee listen to our souls now pleading
that all creation's beauty growing
would comfort body and soul with mending
and peacefulness in our daily sowing.

(A blessing to Debby and Scott Grosse at the opening of Vaughn's nursery (2002)

A Garden of the Heart

Angels of our flowering world
watch our garden delight.
Bring rain and sun and fertile soil
as blossoms find their summer fun.

Bless the flowers with heavenly grace
as each will find new homes
in shaded garden plots and pots
and in a sculptured vase.

Send them forth with deepest love
"my kids" to find a welcome hearth
where wonder will again be born
to mend a broken heart.

Bless dandelions that always shine
as if the sun itself
and though the sky is filled with clouds
brightly show their golden wealth.

Bless zinnias and roses and flowering crab
surrounding yards with color
as praying mantis says her prayer,
rainbows 'mid a world once drab.

Hear this prayer, O angels fair
that I may now enjoy
for in my soul your flowers grow
a field array with joy.

(A prayer for Debbie and Scott at the close of their garden nursery, 2009)

Spirit of Love

Sing your welcome, angels of love
Color the sky with your peace
Open the gates to all above
Let joyful parties never cease.

Dance with Emily, our child dear
Ring the universe with mirth
Holding her close, holding her near
This day is her heav'nly birth.

Circle us round with your healing power
Touching our hearts with your balm
Be present every day and hour
Bring to us a peaceful calm.

When life is shaking and perverse
Lift our eyes to heaven's bliss
Her sweet soul fills the universe
Let sunlight be her kiss.

The blessing of her life on earth
Filled with wonder and with joy
Calls now for us to give new birth
For this earth, our love employ.

God's smile was found in Emily's face
A brief but lovely moment
Now she lives in God's sacred place
A sparkling angel's testament.

Sing your welcome, angels of love
Emily joins your chorus
She now is in your treasure trove
Bringing joy to you from us.

(A tribute to Emily, a young girl who lost her life while crossing the street.
She envisioned how religions can live together in the same household as
she did with Islam and Christianity in the same household.)

An Angel among Us

Catherine Louise Price, an actress turned minister, vivacious and energetic, beauty exuding from every word, every look, every laugh, remains an angel among us.

She was like a rising star whose brightest-of-lights persona was eclipsed at the age of forty-five by the earth's shadow of cancer. During the time when we shared the privileges of ministry, Catherine and I shared life as it came to us. When she first discovered that cancer had presented itself, she kept the disease far in the wings while faith was on center stage. We found many ways of communicating, among them poems and prayers. Included here a poem at the onset of the physical assault and a birthday greeting, the last one I wrote. Another is like a prayer at the time when she lost her hair due to chemotherapy. (To one of them, she responded, "Wow!") The tribute for her memorial service was written to portray her faith that even at death's door, or better, heaven's gates, her faith served all of us and thus made us stronger and more filled with hope, the hope that is God's gift. And so we spoke to one another in a language that was understood, a translation of mysterious matters into simple words, a rhyme where there is no rhyme or reason.

What follows is pastoral care, but let me assure you, its intention was pastoral and, with hope, gave some healing for heart and soul.

Sing to My Heart

Render your song as at Christ's birth
O angels of glory
Sing to my heart as of old
For like shepherds my heart doth quake
O thou angels make me bold
Fill my sky with angelic presence
Tell me to not fear
Your song is more than earth can bear
Travel with me on my pilgrimage
For Bethlehem is not so far away
And miracles do happen as in every age
I kneel before all hallowed mangers bare
The One I love is always there
Child of mercy, walk my walk
Along this desert land
Of which your angels talk
With waters that wash me over again
Set me free from all that captures
Body and Soul in ceaseless pain
Drift with me in the arms of love
Send me forth with Christ who heals
Who blesses, who lives within as above
Sing to my heart as of old
O angels, and attend me with glory.

(Written for Rev. Catherine Price for her birthday, July 31, 2005)

Adorning

How will you adorn me now
How crown my shining barren head
Angels with flowing golden hair
Is there a beauty heaven-sent
Of which I know not?

Earth with its triumphant say
Has little I wish to hear
Amid the speaking of ages
And kingdoms come.

O Angels with your flaxen glow
How am I to know what crown I am given
when what I saw before is driven
away by powers going above and beyond
simple duties of healing?
creating arroyos with flash floods
to burn and scavenge
and replenish this darkened forest
where unchosen tangles have placed my feet
my soul

Lead me, angels of luxurious hair
To the waiting room of God's surprise
Adorn my heart with flowing love
My soul with crowning beauty
Let me see what cannot be seen
know what cannot be known
in the sweetness of caressing wings
the embrace of love stretching beyond
these earthly matters
as God's sacred healing returns me whole.

(Written for Catherine Price as chemotherapy ends)

Sunshine Angels

Sunshine angels with beaming light
create shadows with which I can play
imagining friends in which to delight
sharing unseen worlds along my way.

Hold forth with sparkling eyes to see
and gasping breaths of wonder
that no surprise would ever be
wrenched from me asunder.

Hear sweetness ring from every bell
and dancing through the meadow
for now I know that all is well
beyond all earthly shadow.

My heart a choir from which to sing
an anthem for God's glory
and from your heavenly home do bring
a singing of Christ's story.

Sunshine angels in my change
I find a life that's new
though earth my body rearrange
with love my soul renew.

And so, my angel friends, so near
I'm born again this day
as through my life I'm held as dear
God loves me every way.

(Happy birthday, Catherine, July 31, 2007)

A Tribute

Catherine, Oh Catherine,
just when darkness settled in,
you led us to the tomb,
foreboding and dim,
and called out that light was shining,
empty gloom filled with love from him,
who reached into your heart.

Catherine, Oh Catherine,
though suffering all earth does impose,
your heart went seeking,
found hope which God does disclose,
inviting us to bask with you
in love and relief, renewing our spirits,
our joy, our belief,
once more you spoke,
of love profound.

Catherine, Oh Catherine,
you lifted your face when hymns were sung
to gaze beyond the sky,
where wonder reigns and welcomes home,
where peace at last draws nigh.
You heard again the words of one
who stands on every shore,
"Come, follow me,"
and I will show you more,
now, in God's eternity.
Catherine, Oh Catherine!

(A tribute to Catherine Louise Price for her memorial service, September
27, 2008)

Peace

As Christmas draws near

May the angels who sang at Christ's birth

sing for you in these moments of sorrow.

May they surround you with God's gracious love

and bring you sweet memories on the morrow.

May their wings fan glowing embers of love

as heaven now their soul receives.

May memory ornaments fill your heart

as well as all your Christmas trees.

May angels in a chorus grand

herald news of God's open arm.

May they embrace when all seems cold

his fire of love to keep you warm.

May peace be yours as celebrations

recall past years of wonder and play.

Now may peace be with you and all you love.

(A prayer at a time of grieving)

Mystery

Angels of divine grace
come and refresh my soul
wearied by sudden burdens
that have no language or voice.
Lift my eyes beyond Beyond
that I may enter
where I could not see before
and behold the mystery
of resurrections untold.

(For Jan and Vic Fraccaro)

Inspirational Thoughts

From Inspired Moments

Prayer
Soul Romancing
Beloved
Ice-alations
Meeting Janus
Gardens of Hope
A World Prays
Listen for Angel Songs

Prayer

Angels loving, angels kind
Fold me in God's heart of love
With tender mercy my soul please bind
To peacefulness from heav'n above.

I bring my soul now filled with fear
Before God's majesty divine
Touch with sweetness every tear
Console my grief, O Jesus mine.

Spring rests within my deepest part
I pray that joy will soon burst forth
For I remain your garden plot
My flowering life shows God like worth.

Enfold me on this edge of life
My loving ways surround all way
My heart's wonder meets all strife
Faith, hope, and love come into play.

Fly me to new worlds that wait
Hold me tight in your embrace
Fill my soul as I create
A chapel heart for life's new place.

Angels loving, angels kind
Mend every tear of spirit's woe
For now I give myself and bind
My deepest heart, my body so.

Soul Romancing

When I first saw you
My heart stirred so deeply
Soul yearning
Your eyes soft and gentle, pleading
You spoke, but there was no hearing
I saw your words
Shaped by lips of luxurious fullness
And your contoured body moving
You to me and I to you with eager dancing
So that in our touching
One became another
Warm enveloping
Fragrances within, wafting
Holding without divisions
Melting
One with one
Ecstasy igniting
Until parting
Our fingertips touching
In a struggling good-bye, departing
Sweetness and hope ever lingering.

(Depicts awareness of peace as feminine)

Beloved

How you have moved my heart,
O angels of sweet rapturous love,
lifting my soul with messages
of divine mercy,
sheltering me with holy embrace,
enabling me to see beyond,
beneath all that I call my life.
I move, carried on your wings
that fan heaven's presence
even with my feet embedded in the earth
and my soul immersed in its shadows.

You leave the divine imprint upon me
and I breathe its air,
surrounding me with grace,
delivering me where I most belong,
before I was born and even after,
when I am no longer held by this pilgrimage
over which you have poured your salvation
and called me beloved.

Ice-alations

Wrap this world in miracles,
Oh angels of all, most holy,
Fly with your wings of mercy,
Unfolding myriad blessings,
Reaching hearts untouched,
Warming cold and lonely flesh,
Mortal ice-alations,
Without earth or heaven connections.
Sweep over me,
For I alone meander,
As do iron-cold asteroids
Seeking for places to crash,
Impacts at least,
For small attentions,
Perhaps a little something,
From a garden once known,
Lost by ill-advised seeds sown.
Stand at those rusted gates,
Angels of all most holy
Open them,
Slightly ajar,
A space to squeeze into Eden,
Even a brief moment,
United with all,
Wholeness retrieved.
Wrap my world in miracles.

Meeting Janus

Do you carry a charge of all divine
In this new year that waits before me
O angels of glowing promise
Do you bring peace to this lonely heart of mine?

Tune my soul to hear you sing
Of sweetness forgotten or never known
O angels of all delights
What good news do you have to bring?

Fly me above earth's struggling hold
My feet on sod now barely touching
O angels of lifting joy
Will you point me to new loves untold?

Carry me above all pain and sorrow
My soul set sight on all that's new
O angels of eternity's day
Can you help me know tomorrow?

Breathe through my body, breathe through my mind
Fill me with air from earth's beginning
O angels of infinite love
How will you with all divine my soul thus bind?

Unfold those days that lie ahead
With surprise and wonder fill
O angels of glorious singing
Will you anoint God's blessing on my head?

Wait with me through every day
Wing me through the space of time
O angels of my grandest dream
Will you hold my hand through life's new way?

Gardens of Hope

Skies blemished with missile trails,
pocked and broken earth deserts,
humans kneel in pleading wails,
Invade our troubled lands,
Angel armies!
Such a prayer prevails
in silence,
above screaming sirens
and nightly arms fired.

Angel troops and regiments
give flesh to mercy!
In stone-cold hearts
sculpt images of compassion
from each nation—soul inspired.
Pull from wells of deep desires
waters that heal.
Draw that all may drink
elixirs of Eden's wonders
united as long ago,
companions in Creator walks
through earthly gardens of hope.
Oh angels armed with love
send shock and awe
as it is above!

(This poem was written for the International Society of Poets Convention
and Symposium in Washington DC, August 15-17, 2003. It was added
to the World's Longest Poem for Peace.)

A World Prays
(Regarding the traumas of 2009, 2010)

Draw from rubble of flood and quake
Angels of mercy and care
Lifetimes lost by a single shake
More than souls can ever bear.

Hear fainting cries from rubble rise
Give strength to those above
Their aching bodies, frenzied eyes
As heavy stones they lift and shove.

Would that nature's wildness cease
but more, our wars of greed
that earth itself would be at peace
and labor giv'n to starving need.

Bless the hearts of those who grieve
for we are much the same
to anguish souls, give reprieve
renew life as some remain.

God knows the tongue and native word
of every prayer that's said
Angels bring your merciful sword
to free the wearied heart instead.

Listen for Angel Songs

We will listen for a song of hope
when despair is heavy.

We will listen for a song of joy
when sorrows are shattering.

We will listen for a song of rejoicing
when sadness forces its way.

We will listen for a song of courage
when fears mount up.

We will listen for a song of peace
when life is disturbed.

We will listen for a song of grace
when the world is unforgiving.

We will listen for a song of love
to inspire the way we live.

We will listen for angel songs
to guide through all our years.

INDEX

A

And God's angels gathered round, 40
Angels loving, angels kind, 85
Angels of divine grace, 80
Angels of God's birthing breath, 41
Angels of mercy, cover the world, 69
Angels of our earthenware, 23
Angels of our flowering world, 72
Angels of passionate love, 45
Angels showering mercy, 55
Angels winging through my heart, 63
As Christmas draws near, 79

B

Beginning all beginnings, 25
Bethlehem angels, sing out again, 39
Bundled in infinite mercy, 61

C

Catherine, Oh Catherine, 78
Catherine Louise Price, an actress
    turned minister, 74
Circle me with your dancing, 62
Come fly with me in your angel sky,
    56

D

Did you see it, 57
Do angels fly, 64
Do you carry a charge of all divine,
    89
Draw from rubble of flood and
    quake, 91
Draw near to this heated earth, 70

F

Fashion my heart with lightness, 60
"For a thousand years in thy sight are
    but as yesterday when it is past,
    and as a watch in the night", 46

G

Gathered in the warm embrace of
    presence, 58
Grant your angels spread their wing,
    71
Guide the stars of summer, 27

H

How will you adorn me now, 76
How you have moved my heart, 87

I

I saw you, gracious Angels dear, 24
It was you who brought forth, 48

L

Listen to the wind, 34

M

My heart doth float when you are
    near, 50
My heart was empty, 59

O

O Holy God, 44
O my soul, 12
Over the years when mountains
    seemed insurmountable, 49

R

Render your song as at Christ's birth,
    75
Roll in, thou quiet drifting fog, 29

S

Send watchful care, O angels sweet,
    43
She stood on hilltops, 28
Sing your welcome, angels of love, 73
Skies blemished with missile trails,
    90
Summer angels, 26
Sunshine angels with beaming light,
    77

Sweet angels come, 32

T

thou, 33

W

We will listen for a song of hope, 92
When I first saw you, 86
Wrap this world in miracles, 88

Y

You sweep with lovely colors rare, 31

Edwards Brothers Malloy
Thorofare, NJ USA
March 26, 2013